IRAN

DI ARABI

OMA

GULF STATES

MICHAEL GALLAGHER

W

FRANKLIN WATTS
LONDON•SYDNEY

501336511

Designer Steve Prosser
Editor Simon Adams
Art Director Jonathan Hair
Editor-in-Chief John C. Miles
Picture Research Diana Morris
Map Artwork Ian Thompson

© 2005 Franklin Watts

First published in 2005
by Franklin Watts
96 Leonard Street
London
EC2A 4XD

Franklin Watts Australia
45-51 Huntley Street
Alexandria
NSW 2015

ISBN 0 7496 5810 X

A CIP catalogue record for this book is
available from the British Library.

Printed in Malaysia

Picture credits

Action Press/Rex Features: 31
AKG Images: 16
Sabah Arar/Rex Features: 40
Bettmann/Corbis: 27t, 27b, 28, 33
Bibliothèque Nationale, Paris/Visioars/AKG
Images: 15
British Library, London/HIP/Topham: 21
Burstein Collection/Corbis: 12
Chris Collins/Corbis: 38
Mary Evans Picture Library: 18, 22
Antoine Gyori/France Reportage/Corbis:
front cover t, 13
Sharok Hatami/Rex Features: 30
Image Works/Topham: 11, 25
Keystone/Rex Features: 32
MAI/Rex Features: 37
MGG/Rex Features: 35
Picturepoint/Topham: 8, 24
Popperfoto: 20, 26
Reuters/Corbis: front cover b, 41
P. Michael Rhodes/Picturepoint/Topham: 14
R. Sheridan/Ancient Art & Architecture
Collection: 10, 17
Sipa/Rex Features: back cover, 36, 39
Today/Rex Features: 34
TRH Pictures: 19t
Charles Walker/Topham: 19b

*Every attempt has been made to clear
copyright. Should there be any inadvertent
omission, please apply to the publisher for
rectification.*

IRAN

DI ARAB

OMA

CONTENTS

PEOPLES OF THE GULF

The Persian or Arabian Gulf is a region of stark contrasts. While the Arabian peninsula has always been an arid place, the lands to the north were home to humankind's earliest developed societies.

THE CRADLE OF CIVILISATION

Thousands of years ago, at the neck of the Persian Gulf, life as we know it first took shape. It was here that humans learned to farm and so began to stay in one place throughout the year. Hence, around 3500 BC, the first known city-states emerged in Mesopotamia, a lush, fertile region between the Tigris and Euphrates rivers. Here, too, the first organised warfare took place, as the settlers defended and expanded their territories. Between the fourth and second millennia BC, the Sumerian, Akkadian, Assyrian and Babylonian civilisations fought and flourished in succession. Later, Mesopotamia was colonised by the Turks. Today, we know the region as the largely Arab country of Iraq.

IRAN: A LENGTHY HISTORY

Long before the Arabs arrived, Mesopotamia was ruled by Persia, the country we now call Iran. Under its ruler, Cyrus the Great, the Persian Empire was the biggest in the world, complete with an advanced administrative system. The Persians developed a sophisticated culture; the invasion of Alexander the Great of Macedon between 334-331 BC further enriched this culture with Greek influences. Although Alexander conquered the Persians, their highly developed cultural traditions survived, and by the third century AD, a new dynasty, the Sasanids, was vying for control of the Middle East. The ancient Persian cultural identity has remained important to this day in setting Iran apart from the Gulf's Arab countries to its south and west.

DESERT TRIBES

In other parts of the Gulf, life was very different. In the Arabian peninsula's vast, inhospitable desert, agriculture was usually impossible. For many centuries, Bedouin Arabs led a nomadic existence, tending animals and moving from place to place in a constant search for food and water. These people belonged to no country but only to various tribes. Indeed, kinship ties remain important to the Gulf Arabs today, despite the peninsula's division into modern states such as Saudi Arabia, Yemen and Oman.

The lifestyle of the Bedouin or nomadic Arabs has remained unchanged for centuries.

CROSSROADS OF THE WORLD

With the Gulf's key position between east and west, its peoples have prospered as

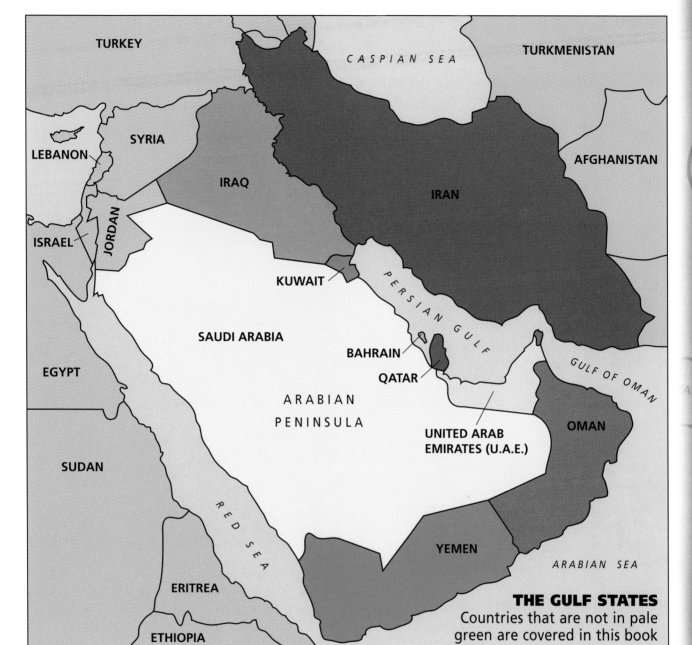

TURKEY

CASPIAN SEA

TURKMENISTAN

SYRIA

LEBANON

AFGHANISTAN

IRAQ

IRAN

ISRAEL

JORDAN

KUWAIT

PERSIAN GULF

SAUDI ARABIA

BAHRAIN

QATAR

GULF OF OMAN

EGYPT

ARABIAN
PENINSULA

UNITED ARAB
EMIRATES (U.A.E.)

OMAN

SUDAN

RED SEA

YEMEN

ARABIAN SEA

ERITREA

THE GULF STATES
Countries that are not in pale
green are covered in this book

ETHIOPIA

merchants, trading with Africa, India, eastern Asia and - later - Europe. For this reason, the Gulf has often absorbed foreign ideas about politics, religion and so on. Yet contact with outsiders, combined with the Gulf's own social, cultural and religious differences, has also brought conflict. Thus for various reasons, life in the different countries of the Gulf has been tainted with violence for as long as anyone can remember.

THE GULF IN ANCIENT TIMES

c3500 BC First urban settlements in Mesopotamia

c1000 BC Flourishing kingdom of Saba in modern-day Yemen enables foreign

influences and trade to enter the Arabian peninsula

550 BC Persian Acheminid Empire established

334–331 BC Invasion of Persia by Alexander the Great

224 BC–AD 651 Persian Sasanid Empire, with its capital at Ctesiphon

on the River Tigris

540–629 Warfare between Sasanid and Christian Byzantine Empires weakens both sides prior to the Muslim expansion

THE BIRTH OF ISLAM

Today, Islam is the dominant faith throughout the Gulf region. But it was introduced to the world by just one man – and in the face of the strongest opposition.

MUHAMMAD'S WORLD

By the 7th century Sasanid Persia and its western neighbour, the Byzantine Empire, were engaged in a long and bitter fight to control Mesopotamia. One consequence of this almost constant warfare was the disruption of overland trade links through the region, which boosted an alternative route through Arabia. Among the beneficiaries of this new trade was a tribe called the Quraysh, which governed Mecca, a small town in the west of the peninsula. The Quraysh also controlled access to the Ka'ba, a pagan shrine at Mecca that pilgrims paid money to enter. But although the Quraysh and a few others were rich and powerful, for most people Mecca remained a brutal and unforgiving place. It was into this town, around the year 570, that the Prophet Muhammad was born.

WORDS FROM GOD

The life of Muhammad ibn Abdallah was an extraordinary one. An orphan, he was raised by his uncle and worked as a merchant for some years. However, when he was about 40 years old, he took to wandering in the desert outside Mecca, deep in thought and contemplation. Islam teaches that, on one such occasion, he was summoned by the Archangel Gabriel to receive the first of many divine communications or revelations. These revelations were later written down to produce Islam's holy text, the Qur'an (also called the Koran). They commanded men to worship the one God, Allah, and to dispense with the corruption, greed and idol worship that was widespread in Mecca.

Muslims believe Muhammad was taken at night by the Archangel Gabriel from Mecca to Jerusalem to ascend into heaven and into God's presence.

YEAR ZERO

Muhammad attracted a small group of supporters, but Mecca's Quraysh rulers did not tolerate him for long, especially when he called for an end to the lucrative Ka'ba pilgrimages. In 622 they attacked him and his followers, forcing them to take refuge 320 km away in Medina. Muslims consider this flight from Mecca, known as the hijra, as the start of their calendar.

UNITED IN FAITH

In Medina, the fledgling Muslim community grew rapidly. Muhammad continued to receive revelations, but he also

proved to be a remarkably successful military tactician, as he and his followers began attacking the Quraysh trade caravans. Their victories – often against all odds – earned them more and more recruits. Before long, Muhammad was made ruler of Medina and in 630 – just eight years after being driven out – he returned to Mecca with 10,000 men, bearing an ultimatum to the Quraysh: surrender and accept Islam, or die. Overwhelmed, the Quraysh gave in. Thereafter, Islam spread throughout most of Arabia, the Ka'ba became a Muslim shrine and the desert peninsula's brutal society was, to some extent, reformed by the divine commands revealed to Muhammad.

In 630 Muhammad rededicated the pagan Ka'ba shrine in Mecca to Allah. Every Muslim tries to visit Mecca and the shrine once in their lifetime.

> **'Know that you are now one brotherhood. Your lives, your property and your honour are sacred and inviolable amongst one another until you appear before your Lord.'**
>
> **Muhammad's command to the Muslims of Arabia**

BIRTH OF ISLAM

610 Muhammad receives the first revelations on Mount Hira, near Mecca

612 Muhammad begins preaching according to the revelations

622 Flight (hijra) of Muhammad and around 70 Muslim families to Medina

624 Muslims defeat the Meccans at the Battle of Badr

627 Battle of the Trench: Muhammad demonstrates his tactical skills by digging a ditch around Medina, successfully defending it against the Meccans

628 Brief truce between the two sides

630 Muhammad returns to Mecca

632 Death of the Prophet Muhammad

ISLAM DIVIDED

Muhammad's death in 632 left Muslims with a dilemma: who should succeed the Prophet to lead their community? Within a few years, the answer that emerged would leave many of his followers feeling betrayed.

ORIGINS OF THE SCHISM

Islam's success turned Arabia from a land of squabbling tribes into a more united religious community. But only two years after his conquest of Mecca, Muhammad died. Muslims were divided over who should take his place. As he had left no sons, some thought it best to appoint one of his closest followers. Others insisted that only a member of Muhammad's family should become caliph (leader). Their champion was Muhammad's devout cousin and son-in-law, Ali. But, amid much deliberation, Abu Bakr - one of Muhammad's most loyal colleagues - emerged as the first caliph before he, too, soon died. Over the next 25 years, two more of the Prophet's close associates were made caliph and each time Ali was passed over.

RETURN OF THE ARISTOCRATS

However the third caliph, Uthman, was controversial. He was related to the Quraysh, the old Meccan ruling tribe, and many thought his kinsmen were more interested in recovering their old power base than in Islam. Among Uthman's opponents was a group called the Kharijites, who sought to recreate the spiritual purity of Muhammad's first Muslim community. In 656 the Kharijites murdered Uthman. Once again, the Muslims had to choose a new leader; this time, they chose Ali.

ALI'S MARTYRDOM

The odds were against Ali from the start. One of Uthman's powerful kinsmen, Muawiyyah, immediately challenged his right to be caliph. The two sides met at the Battle of Siffin in modern-day Iraq. Ali was supported by the Kharijites, who hated Muawiyyah's aristocratic stance. But when Muawiyyah was almost beaten, he called for arbitration in the name of the Qur'an. Ali accepted in good faith. The Kharijites saw this as an act of betrayal, and turned on Ali. In 661 they murdered him and Muawiyyah seized the chance to become caliph, founding the 90-year Umayyad dynasty. Ali's son, Hussein, tried to wrestle the caliphate back, hopelessly outnumbered but determined nevertheless to struggle against what he saw as the wrong done to

A page from a 15th-century Asian manuscript illuminated with scenes from the life of Ali.

his father. At the Battle of Karbala in 680 he, too, paid with his own blood.

A LEGACY OF DIVISION

The martyrdom of Ali and Hussein inspired a new branch of Islam. The Shi'as or 'partisans of Ali' keep their distance from mainstream Sunni Muslims to this day, and Shi'ism is fuelled by an historic sense of injustice. Shi'as believe that there have been 12 imams or leaders, all descended from the Prophet, and that the 12th remains hidden, ready to return to dispense justice. This split between Sunnis and Shi'as has had profound consequences for the Gulf region in modern times.

Every year, Shi'a Muslims gather in Karbala in central Iraq to commemorate the anniversary of the martydom of Hussein, Muhammad's grandson.

THE ASHURA

For Shi'as, the tragedy of Ali and Hussein is not just religious history but a living experience, even today. Few events demonstrate this more powerfully than the Ashura Festival, held each year on the traditional date of Hussein's martyrdom at Karbala in Iraq. Participants weep uncontrollably over his death, and in a ritualistic expression of grief, beat themselves with chains or even cut their own flesh.

SUNNIS AND SHI'AS

632–4 Caliphate of Abu Bakr: his influence prevents some tribes leaving the alliance after Muhammad's death

634–44 Caliphate of Umar ibn al-Khattab:

Muslims expand into Iraq, Syria and Egypt

644 Umar murdered; Uthman is caliph

656 Murder of Uthman; Ali's caliphate disputed

656–60 Civil war rages over the succession to the caliphate

657 Battle of Siffin. Muawiyyah uses his offer of arbitration to depose Ali

661 Ali murdered by Kharijites

680 Shi'as proclaim Hussein as caliph; Hussein killed at Karbala by the Umayyad caliph, Yazid I

13

THE GOLDEN AGE OF ISLAM

Islam's expansion during the 7th century beyond Arabia spelled the end of the Sasanid Empire and quickly led to an age of brilliant progress and unimaginable riches.

PERSIAN COLLAPSE

As early as 637, Muslim Arabs had defeated the Persians at the Battle of Qadisiyyah and moved on to capture their capital, Ctesiphon. Before long, the Sasanid Empire was totally destroyed. However, while Persia now became Muslim, it did not become dominated by the Arabs, unlike most of the Middle East. Indeed, its age-old culture reasserted itself and eventually came to influence the culture of the invaders.

THE NEW BAGHDAD

The resentment of non-Arab Muslims, including Persians, helped to bring about a revolution against Muawiyyah's Umayyad dynasty in 750. The leaders of this uprising established a new Sunni dynasty, the Abbasids. They murdered their predecessors - along with the latest Shi'a pretender to the caliphate - and then built a brand new imperial capital on the River Tigris at Baghdad. The Shi'as now retreated from mainstream politics and society, preferring to look inwards rather than outwards.

Meanwhile, being so close to the heart of the old Sasanid Empire, the Abbasids employed large numbers of Persians and began to follow Persian imperial tradition. Unlike the earlier caliphs, however, they lived in extravagant style: 100,000 architects, and builders worked for 40 years to construct their dazzling new city, which boasted street lighting, fountains and over 700 libraries. Islam, with its ideals of a community that worships with simplicity and equality, had never known such grandeur.

The Mederese Al-Multansariya, the main school in Baghdad built during the Abbasid era.

ABBASID CULTURE

The Abbasids continued to hold the caliphate for 500 years. During their first two centuries they presided over some of the most spectacular advances in human history. Mathematics, physics, law and literature all flourished. Ancient Greek philosophical texts were translated into Arabic, thus keeping alive the works of thinkers such as Aristotle and Plato. At the same time, Islam spread far beyond Arabia

IRAN

DI ARAB

OMA

In 1258 Baghdad was sacked by the Mongols from central Asia, bringing the 500-year-old Abbasid caliphate to an end.

and the Gulf, eventually stretching from Spain in the west to India in the east.

DECLINE AND FALL

Eventually, Abbasid authority declined. For more than 100 years, they ceded real authority to a group of Persian Shi'as, called the Buyids. The Abbasid caliphs later sought protection from a union of Turkish tribes known as the Seljuks. Eventually, Baghdad was sacked by the ferocious Mongol armies of Genghis Khan's son, Hulagu, and the last Abbasid caliph was killed.

HARUN AL-RASHID (736–809)

The son of a caliph and a slave-girl, Harun al-Rashid led Islam into its most glorious period. It was during his glittering reign that Baghdad assumed its legendary position in Arab history, immortalised in the tale of *The One Thousand and One Nights*. His palace was bigger than that of any caliph before him, and he was attended by hundreds of courtiers. An excellent soldier, he waged war against the Byzantines, extracting great riches from their emperor. Yet he was also known as a fair and just ruler, sometimes even going undercover to find out if his subjects were content. After his death, his Abbasid dynasty declined as his sons fought a civil war over the succession.

THE ABBASID DYNASTY

750 Abu al-Abbas defeats the Umayyads, establishing the Abbasid caliphate

754–75 Caliphate of al-Mansur; leading Shi'as persecuted

762 Baghdad founded as new Abbasid capital

786–809 Caliph Harun al-Rashid rules Abbasid Empire during its most glittering period

945 Persian Buyid military dynasty takes over in Baghdad

1055 Seljuk Turks invited to form a military protectorate in Baghdad in order to defend the caliph

1220s Genghis Khan brings Persia under Mongol influence

1258 Mongols under Hulagu sack Baghdad and kill the last caliph, ending Abbasid rule

15

THE LONG STRUGGLE FOR IRAQ

The Mongol invasions began a period of fragmentation throughout the Middle East. When a new imperial order was established 300 years later, it was accompanied by bitter conflict.

ISLAM IN PIECES

After the destruction of Baghdad in 1258, Muslims would never again be united under a single caliph. Instead, by the 16th century, three new empires dominated the Islamic world. One of them, Mogul India, lies outside the scope of this book. But the other two - the Turkish Ottoman and Persian Safavid Empires - would have a long-lasting impact on the Gulf.

POWERFUL RIVALS

The Ottomans based their empire outside the region, in modern-day Turkey, but their territory eventually included parts of modern-day Iraq, Yemen and the Hijaz, the western edge of Arabia that includes Mecca and Medina. The Ottoman leaders, known as sultans, saw themselves as heirs to the old Sunni caliphs of Baghdad. However, at the same time, the Safavids of Persia were constructing a rival empire next door. Its origins owed much to a young boy, Ismail, who in 1501 proclaimed himself shah or king of Persia. Significantly, Ismail also introduced Shi'ism as the official state religion, setting the stage for years of religious warfare.

In 1598 Shah Abbas 'the Great' moved the Safavid imperial capital to the ancient city of Isfahan.

ABBAS THE GREAT

The reign of Shah Abbas I, 'the Great' (1571–1629) saw Persia's Safavid Empire at its most powerful. A great warrior and clever administrator, Abbas brought stability by creating a standing army and expanding Safavid territory, eventually ruling from the River Tigris in the west to the Indus in the east. He cultivated links with Europe and encouraged trade, although he is best remembered for the art and culture that flourished in his splendid capital of Isfahan.

Abbas receives foreign ambassadors in his great palace.

SEE-SAW BATTLE

Ismail turned Persia into the first-ever Shi'a state. He imported Shi'a clergymen, but also claimed semi-divine status for himself. Then, conquering parts of neighbouring Iraq, he forced his new subjects to convert to Shi'ism too. The Sunni Ottomans opposed Shi'a rule and regained control of Iraq in 1534. They also prized Iraq's location on the Tigris and Euphrates rivers, which allow access to the Gulf itself.

The Safavids, for their part, wanted to control Iraq because it was home to the most treasured shrines of Shi'ism, including Karbala, where the would-be caliph Hussein was killed. Hence, in 1624, less than a century after the Ottoman re-occupation, the Safavid shah Abbas the Great reconquered Baghdad, massacring

Sunni inhabitants and forcing yet another Ottoman counter-attack in 1638. This time, the Sunnis would remain in charge.

LONG-TERM CONSEQUENCES

The long years of warfare and forced conversions had a lasting impact on Iraq, whose people became a majority Shi'a population ruled over by Sunnis - a tense situation that has endured to this day. The Safavids left a powerful legacy too. Their dynasty petered out in the early 18th century, and eventually another ruling family, the Qajars, took control. But, unlike Ismail and his descendants, the Qajars did not claim divine status. This gave the Shi'a clerics imported by Ismail far greater leeway to pronounce on matters of Islamic law than was the case in Persia's neighbours, sowing the seeds of revolution even today.

SAFAVID PERSIA

1501 Ismail I leads a revolt against Persia's Turkish Ottoman rulers, founding the Safavid dynasty

1588–1629 Reign of Shah Abbas I, 'the Great', marks the height of Safavid power; the capital moves to Isfahan

1624 Abbas's armies massacre Sunnis in Baghdad

1638 Sultan Murat IV reconquers Baghdad for the Ottomans

1722 Invasion and surrender of Isfahan at the hands of Afghan tribesmen

1736 End of the Safavid dynasty as Turkish Ottoman ruler, Nadir Khan, takes the throne

1794 Qajar dynasty established

EMPIRE BY TREATY

In the industrial era, the Gulf's crucial position between east and west became more important. With Europeans seeking to control the world, even tiny lands assumed a strategic importance. Britain, with its maritime ambitions, drew the borders of today's Gulf states.

THE PIRATE COAST

During the 18th and 19th centuries, the Ottoman Turks maintained their supremacy over much of the Middle East, but on the Gulf coast, things were different. This area lay close to the sea route between Britain - then the world's most powerful country - and India, upon which much of Britain's wealth depended. Britain's Royal Navy patrolled the lower Gulf from the 1770s and later made a pact with the Omanis to stop the French moving in. In 1820, and again in the 1830s and 1853, tired of its shipping being attacked by pirates, Britain forged treaties with the sheikhs, or local tribal chiefs, further up the Gulf coast too.

BRITISH DOMINATION

Towards the end of the century, the European imperial rivalries that would eventually explode into World War One were causing increased tension in the Gulf as the Ottomans had formed an alliance with Britain's powerful adversary, Germany. Britain therefore drew up treaties with all the coastal sheikhdoms in 1892, promising full military protection in return for the right to be the sole foreign influence. The sheikhdoms, or Trucial States as they became known, were the forerunners of today's United Arab Emirates, but they were not the only areas of British involvement. Britain had already set up a permanent military base on the island of Bahrain in 1861 and also took Kuwait under its protection in 1899. For much of the next century, the maritime Gulf would be dominated by Britain.

PROFOUND LEGACY

British patronage had profound consequences for the Arabian side of the Gulf. For one thing, it bestowed unique power upon the sheikhs Britain dealt with. They retained exclusive control over this part of the Gulf, since no other local families could possibly replace them. Over the decades, their descendants too enjoyed

The Persian Gulf and Persia, as mapped by French cartographer Alain Manesson Mallet in about 1720.

Ruling the waves: a British warship lies anchored in the Persian Gulf, 1915.

unchallenged power, setting up hereditary monarchies in which opposition was weak or non-existent. This tradition continued even when their territories became independent: Kuwait in 1961 and Bahrain, Qatar and the United Arab Emirates in 1971. To this day, these countries are still governed by the very same ruling families that made treaties with Britain all those years ago.

KUWAIT

When in 1899 the Ottomans tried to recruit Kuwait's Sheikh Mubarak 'the Great' (ruled 1896–1915) into their empire, he turned to Britain for protection. His Al-Sabah dynasty rules the tiny emirate to this day, but Kuwait is one of the more progressive Gulf monarchies, boasting a lively press and other freedoms. On independence from Britain in 1961, Kuwait established a constitution and an elected parliament. but these democratic institutions have brought tension. In 1976 and again 10 years later, parliament was suspended after challenging Al-Sabah policies. Eventually, and after much protest, parliament was reinstated in 1992.

The Kuwaiti Towers symbolise modern Kuwait.

1798 Treaty between Oman and Britain to counteract Napoleonic France

1820 General Maritime Treaty: Gulf sheikhs renounce piracy following British naval action

1835, 1839 Further temporary truces

1853 Perpetual Maritime Truce consolidates previous agreements and upgrades them to a permanent truce

1861 Britain sets up protectorate over Bahrain

1892 Trucial States become formal British protectorates

1899 Anglo-Kuwaiti agreement

1961 Kuwait independent

2 December 1971 Britain withdraws from the Gulf: the former Trucial States federate to become the United Arab Emirates

SCRAMBLE FOR PERSIA

Beyond the Gulf coast, the British were not the only Europeans with influence. In Persia, the fall of the Safavids left the country weak and divided. Here, Russia too competed for supremacy, much to the anger of Persians themselves.

QAJAR WEAKNESS

The 18th century saw big changes in Persia. Safavid rule came to an end and was eventually replaced by the new Qajar dynasty, which set up its capital in Tehran. However, the Qajars had great difficulty in controlling their kingdom: in the absence of any strong central authority, the clergy imported long ago by Ismail soon assumed greater powers. By the 19th century they were richer, more prestigious and more trusted than the state itself. Eventually, the shah found it difficult even to collect taxes. In desperation he resorted to selling

rights to control Persian industries - known as concessions - to foreign companies.

FOREIGN EXPLOITATION

The main countries to benefit from the shah's weakness were Britain, and Persia's neighbour, Russia. Britain and Russia were rivals for much of the 19th century. Their competition to extract concessions left the country worse off than ever and brought the clerics into direct conflict with the shah. For example, in 1890 the shah sold the entire tobacco trade to an English company. The clerics were so incensed

In 1911 Russian troops invaded northern Persia as British troops invaded the south.

they declared it un-Islamic to buy Persian tobacco until the concession was cancelled. Two years later the shah was forced to back down. But the most damaging concession was granted to another Englishman, William Knox D'Arcy. In 1901 he bought most of Persia's oil rights in return for paying just 16% of any profits. A few years later, big oil discoveries were made. The British government then took control of D'Arcy's company and a major slice of Persia's wealth fell into foreign hands.

DESCENT INTO CHAOS

This foreign exploitation contributed to an uprising in 1905, which led to the creation of the country's first majlis, or assembly. The majlis tried to take control of the granting of foreign concessions from the shah. However, the reformers - including everyone from secular modernisers to the conservative Shi'a clergy - had little in common beside their hatred of the monarchy. A new shah, Muhammad Ali, took advantage of their many divisions to launch a counter-revolution. In the civil war that followed, fighting broke out among the reformers themselves. The European powers sensed a threat to their territorial and oil interests. In 1911 British troops landed in the south, while Russian troops invaded the north. Persia's humiliation was complete.

NASIR AL-DIN SHAH

The long reign of Nasir al-Din Shah (1848–96) sums up perfectly Persia's weakness during the 19th century. Assuming the throne at just 17 years of age, Nasir al-Din had only a small army at his disposal. He found it almost impossible to impose authority over both the local tribesmen and over the powerful Shi'a clergy. As a result, Persia fell into a spiral of debt, corruption and inefficiency, and failed to achieve any significant modernisation. Ironically, one of the things Nasir al-Din did achieve was the establishment of an elite cavalry, the Cossack Brigade, where the man who would one day replace the Qajar dynasty, Reza Khan, started his career.

THE QAJAR DYNASTY

1828 Persia signs Treaty of Turkmanchai to end war with Russia and agrees favourable trade concessions

1857 Britain extracts trade and military concessions and rights over Afghanistan

1890–2 Tobacco crisis: British concession over

the tobacco trade withdrawn after widespread protests

1896 Assassination of Nasir al-Din Shah; succeeded by Muzaffar al-Din Shah

28 May 1901 William Knox D'Arcy wins oil concession, leading to the creation of the

Anglo-Persian Oil Company

5 August 1906 Following huge anti-government protests, the shah signs a decree to establish Persia's first majlis or assembly

31 August 1907 Britain and Russia divide

Persia into spheres of influence

24 June 1908 Majlis attacked by the shah's forces; civil war ensues

17 July 1909 Constitution restored; second majlis sits

1911 Russia and Britain invade Persia

World War One focused European minds on the Gulf as never before, since the Ottomans had entered the conflict on the side of Germany. But their defeat in 1918 – partly thanks to their Arab subjects – ushered in radical changes.

THE ARAB REVOLT

For 500 years, the Ottoman Empire had imposed its order on most of the Arabs in the Gulf and been the superpower of its day. However, when it sided with Germany in World War One (1914-18), it came into conflict with Britain, France and Russia. By now, some Arabs within the empire had become restless. In 1915 the Arab ruler of Mecca and Medina, Sharif Hussein ibn Ali, asked the British to help him get rid of Ottoman rule. In a series of letters to a British official, Sir Henry McMahon, Hussein offered to join the war against the Ottomans. In return, he wanted to be made ruler of a large slice of the Arabic-speaking Middle East, something McMahon appeared to promise in his

The Arab Revolt of June 1916 contributed to the collapse of the Ottoman Empire in October 1918.

THE HASHEMITES: A NOBLE DYNASTY

Sharif Hussein (1856-1931) never inherited a magnificent Arab kingdom but the dynasty he founded, the Hashemites, made its mark nevertheless. According to tradition, the family was descended from the Prophet Muhammad himself. In the 1920s one of Hussein's sons, Faisal, was crowned king of Iraq while another, Abdullah, took the Jordanian throne, which the Hashemites retain to this day. When Hussein proclaimed himself a latter-day caliph he aroused anger among some Arabs and was forced into exile. A third son, Ali ibn Hussein, succeeded him as king of the Hijaz in 1924, before being deposed by ibn Saud, later founder of Saudi Arabia.

replies. By 1916 the deal was struck, and that summer the Arabs rose in revolt. Hussein's forces attacked the Ottomans in Mecca and by September had secured most of the Hijaz. Later, they conquered all the Arab lands up to Damascus in Syria.

IMPERIAL BETRAYAL

For many reasons, including the success of the Arab Revolt, the Ottomans were forced to surrender in 1918 and, like their German allies, they faced a punishing settlement.

One penalty was the loss of their Arab possessions to the victorious powers. Yet - either through a misunderstanding or deliberate deception - Hussein was not to get as big a share of the confiscated land as he had hoped. It emerged that Britain and France had made their own secret deal - the Sykes-Picot agreement - in which they had carved up the Middle East between themselves to create new states such as Iraq and Palestine. Far from becoming independent, many Arabs were now to be ruled by mandate: colonised until their rulers considered them ready for independence. Hussein, meanwhile, became king of the Hijaz, a spiritually significant but otherwise barren desert land.

A FAULTY SETTLEMENT

This break-up of the Ottoman Empire had far-reaching consequences, some of which can still be felt to this day. Although they wanted independence, many Arabs would have preferred to keep the old Ottoman power structure, which was after all an Islamic empire. Now, however, they had to find new identities within the states which took its place. The citizens of these new states often had little in common. Iraq, for example, was forged out of three former Ottoman provinces - Baghdad, Mosul and Basra - and comprised Arabs and Kurds, Christians and Jews, and both Sunni and Shi'a Muslims. Making such a diverse state work would turn out to be an almost impossible task. Most importantly, since many Muslims saw these events as the

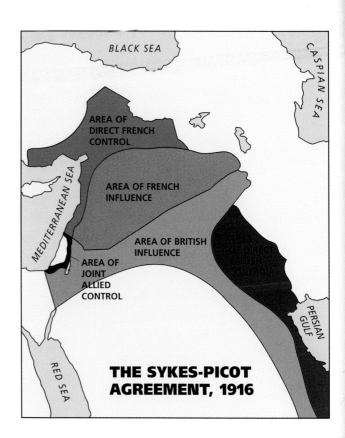

THE SYKES-PICOT AGREEMENT, 1916

'In the blue area France, and in the red area Great Britain, shall be allowed to establish such direct or indirect administration or control as they desire.'

Sykes-Picot Agreement

Muslim world's final capitulation to centuries of European domination, they now began to look harder than ever before for new - and sometimes radical - solutions to their plight.

THE END OF THE OTTOMANS			
August 1914 World War One begins: Ottoman Empire sides with Germany against Britain, France and Russia **14 July 1915** First	letter from Sharif Hussein to Sir Henry McMahon; correspondence continues until 10 March 1916 **June 1916** Arab	Revolt begins **6 July 1917** Arabs capture crucial Red Sea port of Aqaba **1 October 1918** Arab Revolt reaches Damascus, Syria	**11 November 1918** Armistice ends World War One **10 August 1920** Ottomans sign Treaty of Sevres, ceding Arab lands to Britain and France

A KINGDOM IN THE SAND

Among the varied responses to European supremacy was the Wahhabi movement, which stressed a literal understanding of the Qur'an and rejected new interpretations of Islam. In the 20th century, this became the foundation for a new state on the Arabian peninsula.

THE FIRST WAHHABIS

The Wahhabi movement is named after an 18th-century Sunni Muslim, Muhammad Ibn Abd al-Wahhab, who lived in the Najd region of central Arabia. After extensive travel and study, he decided that the Islamic world could only regain its old strength by returning to the simple ideals of the Prophet's original worshipping community and adhering strictly to the Qur'an. His ideas attracted a local chieftain, Muhammad ibn Saud, and they combined to form a movement which, in 1803, captured Mecca. Although the Ottoman rulers soon ousted the Wahhabis, their doctrine remained influential among many Arabian tribes.

WAHHABI CONQUEST

Almost a century later, a descendant of al-Wahhab revived the Wahhabi ideal. Abdul Aziz ibn Saud seized Riyadh in a daring night-time raid in 1902, beginning a long struggle for control of the peninsula. Ibn Saud was both a warrior and a highly skilled statesman, and used marriage to cement alliances with other tribes. At the heart of his project, though, was always the Wahhabi teaching, which gave his leadership a special quality in the eyes of his followers. His forces soon controlled the entire Najd region. In 1924 they ejected Sharif Hussein and his son Ali from the Hijaz, thus capturing Islam's most holy places, Mecca and Medina. The British, who cared little about who ruled Arabia's vast interior so long as their coastal alliances were unaffected, agreed a treaty

Abdul Aziz ibn Saud (front row, left), creator of the unified state of Saudi Arabia in 1932.

with ibn Saud. Consequently, his gains stopped short of such territories as Qatar and the Trucial States. In 1932 ibn Saud united all his possessions into a single kingdom bearing his name: Saudi Arabia.

STRUGGLE TO SURVIVE

Today, we think of the Saudis as fabulously rich, because of their oil industry, but to begin with their kingdom was very poor indeed. Oil extraction did not begin properly until 1947 and there was no other economy to speak of, other than income from the thousands of Muslims making the annual pilgrimage to Mecca. The kingdom was also tangled up in disputes

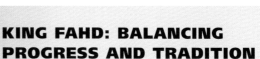

Saudi Arabia has the largest oil and natural gas reserves in the world, bringing it great wealth.

with its neighbours, most notably Yemen and Qatar, over contested territory, since there had never been any formal borders in the desert sands before. Even so, ibn Saud earned legitimacy among his new subjects, thanks to his reputation for fair and judicious rule. True to the Wahhabi ideal, his new state was strict in its adherence to conservative Sunni values and governed according to the Shari'a (Islamic) law. Equally important to many was the kingdom's political credibility: unlike a number of its neighbours, its creation owed nothing to western European powers.

KING FAHD: BALANCING PROGRESS AND TRADITION

King Fahd (born 1923) trod a cautious line in difficult times. When he came to power in 1982, oil revenues were plummeting, forcing him to introduce austerity measures to a society that took wealth for granted. With a personal fortune estimated at $18 billion, though, he endured rising political resentment and religious dissent. Ever the diplomat, he responded with limited constitutional reforms. But he also appealed to conservatives by invoking the House of Saud's Islamic legitimacy, thus keeping a tight grip on power.

SAUDI ARABIA

15 January 1902 Ibn Saud conquers Riyadh

13 October 1924 Ibn Saud takes control of Mecca

20 May 1927 Treaty of Jiddah between Britain and the Saudis

23 September 1932 Formal creation of Saudi Arabia

20 May 1934 Taif agreement establishes border between Saudi Arabia and Yemen; not formally recognised by the Yemenis, who claim loss of three border provinces

9 November 1953 Death of Ibn Saud

25 March 1975 King Faisal shot dead by his nephew

1 January 1996 after suffering a stroke, King Fahd hands day-to-day rule to Crown Prince Abdullah

25

THE PAHLAVI SHAHS

For a century and a half, the clergy's strength had threatened to eclipse Persia's monarchy. But in 1925, a new shah took the throne. Now, state power was applied ruthlessly to deprive the religious establishment of its influence.

ENFORCED WESTERNISATION

Reza Khan Pahlavi was a colonel in Persia's most elite cavalry brigade and determined to end his country's weakness under the Qajar shahs. In 1921 he led a coup d'etat, forcing the shah to appoint a new prime minister, Sayyid Zia Tabatabai, who in turn made Reza commander-in-chief of the armed forces. Over the next four years, Reza accumulated more and more political power, forcing Tabatabai to resign and securing the throne for himself and his heirs. Reza Shah's rule was effective but highly autocratic. He imposed his authority by using the army to suppress minority groups. He silenced opposition from the majlis by reducing it to a mere rubber-stamp assembly. And he dramatically undermined the Shi'a clergy, introducing a raft of western-style secular reforms such as giving civilian judges supremacy over their religious counterparts. In 1935 he sought to erase Persia's Muslim heritage by renaming the country Iran, or 'land of the Aryans', a title that reflected its ancient, pre-Islamic past.

WARTIME INVASION

To Reza Shah, these were measures necessary to modernise Iranian society and so end its humiliation by European powers. To his critics, they were only crude devices to sustain his despotic rule. Crucially, he could not gain control over the British company that produced most of Iran's oil. Instead, he forged links with Britain's World War Two enemy, Nazi Germany. As a result, Britain and the Soviet Union invaded Iran in 1941 and forced him to abdicate in favour of his son, Muhammad Reza.

THE NEW REGIME

With Reza Shah gone, many of the groups he had suppressed tried to regain their former powers. In 1951 one of his former opponents, Muhammad Mossadegh, became prime minister, promising to restrict the new shah's powers. Mossadegh was also a strong nationalist: his solution to British ownership of the Iranian oil industry

Reza Khan Pahlavi, shah of Iran from 1925–41.

MUHAMMAD REZA SHAH

Educated in Switzerland and at the elite Tehran Military College, Muhammad Reza (1919–80) remained detached from his subjects. When he succeeded his father as shah in 1941, he was faced with more than a decade of serious unrest, including an attempt on his life. Proud and strong-willed, he did little to endear himself to his subjects and his critics, preferring to draw parallels between his rule and that of ancient Persian emperors such as Cyrus the Great. He even assumed the title *aryamehr* or 'light of the Aryans'. Despite – and perhaps because of – his grandeur, few shed any tears for Muhammad Reza Shah when he was deposed in 1979. He died in exile in Egypt the following year.

Muhammad Mossadegh (1882–1967)

was to nationalise it. In protest, Britain launched a boycott of Iranian oil, plunging the country into debt. By now the Cold War was in full swing and the USA was alarmed at this latest threat to western influence in the Gulf. In 1953 its agents plotted with Muhammad Reza to stage a coup against Mossadegh. Thereafter, and again with US and British help, the shah clamped down hard on dissent. Britain's oil concession was restored, the majlis suppressed and a new and notorious secret police, the Savak, arrested and tortured opponents. Like his father, the shah cultivated the military, buying enormous quantities of western arms. Like his father, too, he would ultimately push his enemies too far and reap the consequences.

THE PAHLAVI DYNASTY

21 February 1921 Reza Khan Pahlavi marches on Tehran, forcing Tabatabai's government on the incumbent shah

13 December 1925 Reza Khan Pahlavi

elected with the title Reza Shah

1935 Persia is renamed Iran

7 January 1936 Women banned from wearing the veil

25 August 1941 USSR and Britain invade Iran

16 September 1941 Reza Shah abdicates in favour of his son, Muhammad Reza Pahlavi

29 April 1951 Mossadegh nationalises oil industry

19 August 1953 Mossadegh deposed in western-backed coup

FROM KING TO COUP IN IRAQ

The state of Iraq was an artificial creation, carved out of three quite distinct former Ottoman provinces. After a violent anti-colonial uprising, Britain hoped that its interests would be protected by installing a friendly king. But the Hashemite monarchy was as ill-founded as the state itself.

BRITAIN'S DILEMMA

To the British, after World War One the new Iraqi state was a vital link in Britain's overland route to India. Britain therefore intended to retain control of the region. But in June 1920, news that they would do so was greeted with an armed uprising that claimed thousands of lives. To overcome the opposition, Britain therefore turned to an old ally. Faisal, the son of Sharif Hussein, had commanded the Arab Revolt in 1916. Now, he was invited to become Iraq's first king

King Faisal of Iraq, seen here at the Versailles Peace Conference of 1919 that ended World War One, was offered the Iraqi throne by the British.

DISUNITED KINGDOM

Faisal's recruitment represented a desperate attempt at nation-building in a country whose people had little in common. With Kurds in the north, Shi'as in the south and significant Christian and Jewish communities, Iraq was an ethnic and religious melting pot. The installation of a ruler who was foreign to all its peoples seemed to be asking for trouble. King Faisal did his best to hold the country together, with the result that in 1932 the British granted Iraq formal independence. However this was more symbolic than real, for Britain continued to pull the strings. When Faisal died just a year later, any stability that Iraq had enjoyed soon gave way to chaos.

CRISIS POINT

Faisal was succeeded by his son, Ghazi, a young man who displayed little interest in the throne and who was killed in a car crash six years later. The throne now passed to a three-year-old child, Faisal II, who ruled in name only for years under a regent. Lacking a determined monarch, Iraqi politics descended into chaos, with a series of weak, squabbling governments, all headed by minority Sunni Arabs, and periodic bouts of intercommunal violence.

The country's enduring domination by Britain sparked widespread unrest, resulting in a series of military coups between 1936 and 1941, the last of which installed a nationalist, Rashid Ali al-Gailani, as premier. Like Reza Shah in Iran, Rashid Ali leaned towards Nazi Germany. Like Iran, Iraq's hostility to Britain at a time when it

was fighting for its life against the Nazis led to invasion. In May 1941 British troops threw out Rashid Ali's regime, and occupied Baghdad for the remainder of World War Two. Faisal II and his regent were put back on the throne, but the Iraqi monarchy was forever tainted by its dependence on a foreign colonial power. Seventeen years later, a military coup led by Abdul Karim Kassem overthrew the monarchy and led to the deaths of Faisal and many of his advisers.

ABDUL KARIM KASSEM: IRAQ'S FIRST DICTATOR

Brigadier Kassem (1914-63) led the 1958 coup that took the life of Iraq's king, but he rapidly discovered the difficulties of ruling such a disparate state himself. Initially he used the communists for support, but was forced to ditch them as they began to compete for power. He forged links with the Soviet Union, but alienated those Iraqis who wanted a pro-Arab state. Later, he tried to solve the problem of Iraq's restless Kurdish minority. However, when this failed the Kurds mounted a two-year rebellion Kassem was unable to quell, and which ultimately contributed to his own overthrow and death in 1963.

IRAQ: KINGDOM AND REPUBLIC

25 April 1920 Iraq placed under British protectorate; Faisal I becomes king

21 March 1925 'Organic Law' formalises the Hashemites as Iraq's hereditary ruling family

3 October 1932 Formal independence from Britain

8 September 1933 Death of Faisal I

4 April 1939 Death of King Ghazi

1 April 1941 Coup installs government of Rashid Ali

2 May 1941 British military action against Iraq

14 July 1958 Brigadier Abdul Karim Kassem topples the monarchy in a military coup

7 October 1959 Saddam Hussein involved in unsuccessful attempt to kill Kassem

8 February 1963 Kassem overthrown by military; Colonel Abdul Salam Arif installed as president

16 April 1966 Following Arif's death, his brother, Abdul Rahman, takes over Iraqi leadership

17 July 1968 Ba'ath Party takes power

16 July 1979 Saddam Hussein becomes president and commander-in-chief of Iraq and purges Ba'ath Party

Despite growing prosperity and attempts to reform society, Iran's Pahlavi dynasty faced growing opposition in the 1970s. By the end of that decade, Iranians had thrown out both the shah and his western secular culture.

THE WHITE REVOLUTION

After 1953, Muhammad Reza Shah ruthlessly enforced his rule in Iran, using torture and censorship to suppress all opposition. Even so, the shah failed to placate his many critics. In 1963 he therefore launched his so-called White Revolution. This was a series of initiatives offering limited land reforms, improved literacy and economic growth. In some respects, the project did produce results. However, it also boosted foreign investment, undermined traditional industries and further diminished the Shi'a clerics' role in education. Later, the shah scrapped Iran's pretence at democracy by imposing a one-party state. Opposition to his rule became more vocal than ever, and by the late 1970s, the country was gripped by strikes and mass demonstrations.

RISING REVOLT

The opposition represented a broad spectrum of Iranian society, from secular socialists to devout Muslims. Increasingly, though, the Shi'a religious establishment asserted itself over the other elements thanks to its historical role in opposition to the state. In 1978 Iran witnessed its biggest-ever demonstrations, calling for an end to the shah's corrupt rule, independence from foreign interference in Iranian affairs and an Islamic government. It was clear that the uprising could not be suppressed. Everybody, it seemed - young and old, rich and poor - had had enough of the hated monarchy. In January 1979 Muhammad Reza Shah and his family fled the country, never to return.

RETURN OF THE AYATOLLAH

The clergy now stepped up its grip on the revolution while one man emerged to take the lead. Ruhollah Khomeini was a senior Shi'a religious leader, or ayatollah, who had been exiled by the shah 15 years earlier and was living in France. Although by now an

The Ayatollah Khomeini greets children on his return to Iran, February 1979.

old man, his spiritual credentials and past opposition to the regime made him astonishingly popular. When he flew into Tehran in February 1979, more than one million people greeted him.

THE ISLAMIC STATE

Under Khomeini, the revolution swept away the shah's government, and set up an Islamic Revolutionary Council to run the country. In March a referendum massively backed an Islamic Republic. Suddenly Iran changed from a westernised, secular state to a nation run by Shi'a clerics. Everything, from dress codes to television, was governed by Khomeini's version of Islam. In a series of highly popular moves, the new government addressed inequalities in wealth and seized key industries. After centuries, Iranians had taken control of their own destiny. More worryingly for the outside world, Khomeini's regime also began to preach a virulent hatred of the west and to call for other countries to stage their own Islamic revolutions.

> '*In Islam, the legislative power and competence to establish laws belong exclusively to God Almighty.*'
>
> **Ayatollah Khomeini**

MUHAMMAD KHATAMI: REVOLUTIONARY REFORMER

Muhammad Khatami (born 1943) became the Islamic republic's fifth president in 1997, attracting its youthful electorate with promises of social reform. Previously a little-known cleric, his fresh ideas offered an alternative to the ultra-conservatism of the ayatollahs, which the young in particular had tired of. Faced with stiff opposition, his actual achievements were modest: newspapers that supported him were obstructed or closed down, and many of his followers ended up in jail. Yet most experts agree that Iran will have to accept many of Khatami's pioneering changes.

THE IRANIAN REVOLUTION

26 January 1963 White Revolution commences

5 June 1963 Arrest of Ayatollah Khomeini as demonstrations are brutally crushed by the Savak secret police; Khomeini is later exiled

September 1978 Demonstrations and strikes in Iran; martial law imposed

16 January 1979 Shah and his family flee Iran

1 February 1979 Ayatollah Khomeini

returns to Iran

1 April 1979 Islamic republic proclaimed

4 November 1979 US embassy in Tehran seized; 52 taken hostage; hostage-takers demand return of shah from

USA to face trial

27 July 1980 Shah dies of cancer in Egypt

20 January 1981 US hostages released

3 June 1989 Death of Ayatollah Khomeini

31

WAR ACROSS THE GULF

No sooner had the clerics taken power in Iran than a threat emerged to their rule. This time, the enemy was neither the shah nor the west, but the Iraqis under their new leader, Saddam Hussein.

SADDAM HUSSEIN: IRAQ'S BRUTAL MAN OF WAR

From his earliest involvement with the Ba'ath Party, Saddam Hussein (born 1937) was known as a ruthless individual. Years of working in secret while the party was banned gave him an added paranoid streak. His regime relied heavily on friends and kinsmen from his native town, Tikrit, although he thought nothing of ordering their arrest and execution if they aroused his suspicions. Civilians, too, were terrorised into compliance. There was, though, poetic justice for Saddam: his inner circle became so obedient to him that, in the end, nobody dared warn him that he faced certain defeat by the United States.

IRAQ'S OPPORTUNITY

In the immediate aftermath of the Islamic revolution, Iran was in turmoil and its economy and armed forces in disarray. Over its western border, the end of the monarchy in Iraq had, in 1968, ushered in an Arab nationalist party called the Ba'ath. In 1979, just as the new Iranian regime was finding its feet, this party had been taken over by an ambitious and ruthless politician. Like all previous Iraqi rulers, Saddam Hussein was battling with a disunited country in which Kurds, Shi'as and others were at odds with a Sunni regime. In Iran's confusion, he saw an opportunity to overcome these weaknesses and earn a notable victory for his leadership.

A HISTORY OF CONFLICT

Saddam Hussein had other motives for war too. Tensions had been high for some years over Iran's help for the Kurdish rebellion in Iraq, and the two countries also had an historical dispute over ownership of the strategic Shatt al-Arab waterway that lay between the two countries. Most importantly, Iraq had been watching the Islamic revolution in Iran with alarm. Saddam feared Iran's declared intention of exporting its revolution to its neighbours, especially since more than half the Iraqi population was, like the Iranian people, Shi'a Muslim. In September 1980 the first shots rang out across the Shatt al-Arab.

STALEMATE

The Iraqis expected a quick and easy victory over their disorganised enemy. They opened

DI ARAB

OMA

In the early stages of the war, Iraqi troops in Soviet-made tanks attempted to seize vital ports and oil refineries in southern Iran.

up a 500-km front, bombing oil refineries and moving swiftly into Iranian territory. Yet the Iranians, true to their Shi'a culture of martyrdom, proved willing to sacrifice themselves in huge numbers to defend their Islamic state. They reversed early Iraqi successes before being, in turn, repelled themselves. It soon became clear that neither side could make a breakthrough. The war settled into an uneasy stalemate, although it took an alarming turn when both sides began attacking shipping in the Gulf.

OUTSIDE HELP

The outside world, shocked at the threat to its oil supplies, now became embroiled in the conflict. Although fearful of Saddam Hussein's Iraq, few wanted to see an Iranian victory. Led by Saudi Arabia, other states in the Gulf peninsula gave financial aid to Iraq, while the west, though officially neutral, supplied weapons. Yet what the Iranians lacked in firepower they made up for in religious zeal. For almost a decade this tragic, destructive and ultimately futile conflict rumbled on. By the time it ended in a ceasefire in 1988, it had cost hundreds of thousands of lives.

THE IRAN–IRAQ WAR

13 June 1975 Algiers Agreement between then-Vice-President Saddam Hussein and Shah of Iran settles Shatt al-Arab waterway dispute and ends Iranian support for Kurdish rebellion

1977–9 Anti-government demonstrations by Iraqi Shi'a

4 September 1980 Iran shells Iraqi border towns

17 September 1980 Iraq cancels 1975 treaty with Iran

22 September 1980 Iraq first attacks Iran

25 May 1981 Gulf states form Gulf Co-operation Council (GCC) to protect themselves against possible escalation of Iran–Iraq war

16 March 1988 Iraqi chemical attack on its own Kurdish civilians in Halabjah

20 July 1988 Iran accepts United Nations resolution 598 ceasefire

11 September 1990 Diplomatic relations restored between the two countries

OPERATION DESERT STORM

Kuwait's existence had never been accepted by its neighbour, Iraq. In 1990 Saddam Hussein invaded the tiny state. As Kuwait's allies prepared to retaliate, the stage was set for the 'Mother of all Battles'.

SADDAM'S MOTIVES

In 1990 Iraq was an impoverished nation. A decade of war against Iran had left it heavily in debt, and one of its biggest creditors was Kuwait. That summer, enraged that high Kuwaiti oil production was keeping down the price of his own exports, Saddam Hussein massed a huge force on the border dividing the two countries. On 2 August 1990, the Iraqis attacked, securing a rapid victory over their hopelessly outgunned enemy. Appealing to the Iraqis' sense of history, Saddam annexed Kuwait, declaring it to be his country's long-lost 19th province.

WORLD CONDEMNATION

The invasion presented a serious crisis to the international community. One-fifth of the world's total oil supplies were now in the hands of an unpredictable dictator. The west and its Gulf allies feared that Iraq could go further and attack Saudi Arabia. When United Nations' sanctions failed to end Saddam's occupation, the USA began to assemble a military taskforce. They were careful to build international support for their actions, especially from their Cold War adversary, the Soviet Union. In all, 29 nations, including several Arab states, joined the international coalition against Iraq.

Iraqi trucks and supplies lie abandoned alongside the road to Basra after Operation Desert Storm.

RAPID VICTORY

At the beginning of 1991 500,000 allied troops were ready for action in the Gulf. Saddam Hussein remained defiant. When last-ditch peace attempts failed, the US-led coalition launched Operation Desert Storm to liberate Kuwait. With the latest hi-tech weaponry, its superiority was immediately apparent; most of Saddam's forces were poorly equipped conscripts. Commencing with a six-week air attack, the allies moved to a lightning ground war. Saddam tried to escalate the conflict by attacking the Arabs' old foe, Israel, but the Israelis resisted the temptation to reply, as this would have provoked some Arab states to take Iraq's side. The coalition held together and, after just 100 hours of ground fighting, achieved its objective.

DIFFICULT AFTERMATH

Kuwait was free, but at a colossal price. The number of Iraqis killed in this Gulf War is unknown but it was certainly in the tens of thousands. And, despite 'pinpoint-accuracy' missiles and bombs, civilians were among the dead. By contrast, the coalition sustained only minimal casualties. In Kuwait itself, the Iraqis left a trail of damage that included the destruction of three-quarters of the country's oil wells. The Gulf War had its political cost too. The decision of some Arab states to join a war against one of their own number caused lasting rifts

NAMING THE WARS

The first war to be called the Gulf War was the 1980–88 war between Iran and Iraq. In 1991 the name was applied to Operation Desert Storm; the earlier conflict then became known as the Iran–Iraq War. With yet another war against Iraq in 2003, many people now talk about the 1st and 2nd Gulf Wars.

within the Middle East, while the presence of non-Muslim American troops in Saudi Arabia - the land of Islam's holiest places - started a backlash against the west that continues to this day. Among those who condemned the 'infidel' presence was Osama bin Laden.

Osama bin Laden (born 1957), leader of al-Qaeda.

YEMEN

Yemen is that rarest of things on the Arabian peninsula – a relatively poor country. It is also Arabia's only republic. Its recent history is one of division and civil war, accompanied by lengthy squabbles with Saudi Arabia. Yet, against all the odds, it has survived.

DIVISON AND UNITY

Throughout much of the 20th century, Yemen was split into two impoverished states, north and south. In the north, a war between monarchists and republicans produced the Yemeni Arab Republic, which was traditionalist and conservative. But the south, known as the People's Democratic Republic of Yemen, was the Arab world's only Marxist state. Its capital, Aden, was once a British protectorate and a stopping-off point for western shipping, but after independence, the country became a close ally of the Soviet Union. However, South Yemen's leaders quickly

The port of Aden (pictured), was once a strategic British colony on the main shipping route to India.

fell out and descended into violence, both between themselves and with the neighbouring north. Finally, as the Cold War drew to a close, South Yemen found itself with neither money nor international friends, and it was forced to unify with the north in 1990.

AN UNRULY NEIGHBOUR

Since then, the unitary Republic of Yemen has had a difficult existence. It has suffered strained relations with its nearest neighbours in the Gulf and across the Red Sea in Africa. An old dispute with Saudi Arabia has continued to rumble on over three disputed border provinces, while during the Gulf War, both Kuwait and Saudi Arabia were enraged by Yemen's support for Saddam Hussein. The richer countries cut off financial aid to Yemen and deported Yemeni migrant workers.

CIVIL WAR

The Republic of Yemen is governed from the old northern capital, Sanaa, and the north remains, as it always was, more powerful and populous. However, Yemeni oil reserves are mainly in the south, a source of ongoing tension between the two halves. Crucially, their armed forces were never merged, and in 1994, only four years after unification, the south tried to secede, sparking a brief civil war in which northern forces besieged Aden. Still smarting over Yemen's behaviour during the Gulf War, some of its neighbours actively assisted the separatists. However, their efforts came to nothing and the unified Republic of Yemen overcame its enemies, at home and abroad.

GUERRILLA HIDEOUT

To add to its troubles, Yemen has recently become known as a sanctuary for violent extremists claiming to act in the name of Islam. Yemen is still a largely tribal society, and its remote, mountainous interior is difficult for government forces to patrol. In October 2000, al-Qaeda suicide attackers rammed an American warship, the USS *Cole*, in the port of Aden, killing 17 sailors and causing millions of dollars in damage. Since then, Yemen has been a key area in the United States's so-called 'war on terror', and its government has co-operated in trying to root out militants, although with limited success.

USS Cole *on a salvage ship after being attacked and damaged by al-Qaeda agents in Aden in 2000.*

YEMEN

1962 Yemeni Arab Republic established; civil war between royalists supported by Saudi Arabia and republicans supported by Egypt

30 November 1967 South Yemen declares independence from Britain

1 December 1970 South Yemen

renamed People's Democratic Republic of Yemen

1972 Border clashes between North and South Yemen

13 January 1986 Violent power struggle begins in South Yemen

22 May 1990 The two countries unite as the

Republic of Yemen

May 1994 Civil war between north and south; southern separatists declare Democratic Republic of Yemen

7 July 1994 Aden captured by government forces

1995 Yemen clashes with Eritrea over

disputed island

October 2000 Suicide bombers attack the USS *Cole* in Aden; bomb attack on British embassy in Sanaa

October 2002 The *Limberg* oil tanker badly damaged off coast of Yemen in suspected al-Qaeda attack

SADDAM HUSSEIN TOPPLED

President George Bush Sr wanted the Gulf War to be the start of a new order in the Middle East, led by the USA and its allies. But in Iraq, Saddam Hussein continued to threaten US interests. Then came 9/11, the suicide attacks on the USA of 11 September 2001.

The World Trade Center in New York under attack by al-Qaeda on 11 September 2001.

NO PURSUIT

As Iraqi troops retreated from Kuwait, US President Bush assumed that, because Saddam Hussein had been humiliated, the Iraqi leader would be removed from power by his enemies at home. Consequently, the USA and its allies saw no point in pursuing Saddam's shattered army all the way to Baghdad. In any case, the coalition against Iraq would not have approved such action. Instead, the Americans urged Iraqi Kurds, Shi'as and others to rise up against the Ba'ath regime to obtain freedom and democracy.

SADDAM SURVIVES

Saddam's enemies were only too keen to mount rebellions but they expected the USA to give them more than just encouraging words. When it became clear that no western military backing was on its way, the Iraqi regime cracked down ruthlessly on its opponents. Thousands died and some two million Kurds fled their homes. By the end of 1991 it was clear that Saddam had survived.

The next decade was one of constant tension and suffering. The United Nations imposed a trade embargo on Iraq, leading to as many as 500,000 civilian deaths through disease and malnutrition. Saddam also repressed minority groups and, in an attempt to protect them, Britain and the USA enforced 'no-fly zones' on Iraqi military aircraft in the north and south of Iraq. But there were frequent violations, while claims that Saddam had reneged on his obligations under the Gulf War ceasefire led to periodic air strikes against him. Despite all of this, Saddam retained an iron grip on power. In 1998 he refused to allow the return of United Nations inspectors sent to dismantle his most dangerous weapons projects. The US leadership wondered how to conclude the unfinished business of 1991.

SHOCK AND AWE

The answer came after 11 September 2001. With the al-Qaeda suicide attacks on New York and Washington, the USA determined to root out those it suspected of plotting

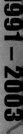

After US forces occupied Iraq in April 2003, all statues of Saddam Hussein were toppled.

against it. President George W Bush – son of the first President Bush – convinced supporters that Saddam Hussein was a prime threat. His allies were deeply split by the decision and few signed up to his new coalition. Nevertheless, using a lightning attack strategy known as 'shock and awe', the USA, Britain and others invaded Iraq in 2003. Within weeks, Saddam's regime was toppled. Many Iraqis were overjoyed to be free of a tyrant but many also bitterly resented foreign military interference. After the war was over, Iraq descended into near anarchy. Much of the violence was directed at western troops, who themselves felt 'shock and awe' at their hostile reception by the people they had just helped to liberate.

SADDAM AND THE BUSHES

The loathing between Saddam Hussein and the Bush presidency was deep and personal. George W Bush never forgot the fact that, while his father was voted out of the White House after Operation Desert Storm, the dictator stayed in power to taunt him. For his part, Saddam felt betrayed by George Bush Sr, the man who had sold him arms to fight Iran but then turned against him over Kuwait. Saddam showed his anger by requiring guests at Baghdad's al-Rashid hotel to wipe their feet on an image of his foe.

THE FALL OF SADDAM

March–April 1991 Uprisings in north and south of Iraq suppressed by Saddam's troops

10 April 1991 USA orders Iraq to end all military activity in Kurdish areas

14 April 1995 UN 'oil-for-food' programme allows limited oil exports in order to buy essentials

31 October 1988 Iraq ends co-operation with UN weapons inspectors

11 September 2001 Massive suicide attacks on US cities; President George W Bush calls for regime change in Iraq

20 March 2003 Start of US-led war on Saddam Hussein;

bombing campaign followed by ground invasion from Kuwait

9 April 2003 US forces enter Baghdad

14 December 2003 Saddam Hussein captured in Tikrit

OLD ELITES, NEW DEMANDS

The Gulf entered the 21st century as a region in transition. Many of its leaders, though traditionally wary of reform, were moving towards democracy. The future stability of this most volatile zone may depend less on outsiders than on its own inhabitants.

IRAQ: A DIFFICULT REBIRTH

In the aftermath of the 2003 invasion of Iraq, the Gulf stood at a crossroads. Its western patrons had once let dictatorships flourish but now the USA and its allies justified their military action by claiming to have started a democratic revolution. Early results were not promising. In Iraq, secular Ba'athists and Islamic militants soon united against a common enemy. Within months, guerrilla resistance had claimed more US soldiers than the combat itself, and an even greater number of Iraqi lives. As the British had decades before, the Americans decided to hand power over to a friendly regime and hope for the best.

ARABIA: POPULAR DISCONTENT

The rigid monarchies of the Gulf were also experiencing pressure for change. Better education had brought rising demands for involvement in their tightly controlled politics as their youthful populations grew restless. In Bahrain, the majority Shi'a community protested against exclusion and discrimination against them while on the

US troops patrol the streets of Baghdad, 2004.

Arabian mainland, unemployment added to the clamour for change. Some accused the millions of expatriate workers of stealing jobs. Others attacked the governing elites. Critics said the 'pampered princes' were corrupt and self-seeking and that their power depended on un-Islamic friendships with the west. Among the dissidents were supporters of the Saudi exile, Osama bin Laden, who were blamed for a string of bomb attacks, mostly on foreigners.

TACTICAL RETREAT

In response, some Gulf states began to meet their critics' demands. Saudi Arabia's King Fahd set up a basic parliament. Although this had only advisory powers and was appointed rather than elected, it was radical indeed for a country that used to claim the Qur'an alone was its constitution. Kuwait, which had dragged its feet over reintroducing a parliament after the 1990 Iraqi invasion, also began to introduce reforms. Even revolutionary Iran was tempted for a while by the moderate reforms of President Muhammad Khatami. Throughout the Gulf, efforts were made to create more jobs to prevent serious unrest.

THE FUTURE

For now, the Gulf remains a place of elite monarchies and radical republics, of political turbulence and ethnic and religious faultlines, and of great resentment over foreign influences. This should come as no surprise, given the region's history of glorious wealth, colonial humiliation and Islamic schism. On top of all this, the Gulf is likely to receive ever more global attention as other sources of oil dry up and as the west pursues its 'war on terror' in the region. Yet if the recent pattern of events continues, the people of the Gulf can at least expect to make more of their own decisions in future – and perhaps, to come to terms with the past.

Prince Saud al-Faisal of Saudi Arabia (born 1940) struggles to direct his country's future.

> **'Our region has suffered more than its share of war and turmoil.'**
>
> **Saudi Foreign Minister Prince Saud al-Faisal speaking in 2003**

PROGRESS AND REFORM

26 August 1975 Bahraini parliament suspended

29 August 1976 Emir of Kuwait dissolves national assembly for the first time

1995 Violent protests by Bahraini Shi'as over Sunni political domination

25 June 1996 Bombing of Khobar Towers military complex in Dhahran, Saudi Arabia; 19 Americans killed

12 May 2003 Osama bin Laden's al-Qaeda network blamed for bomb attacks on expatriate workers in Saudi Arabia, which kill 35

15 June 2003 Demonstrators clash with security forces in Mecca

GLOSSARY

Annex Formal integration of one state's territory into another, usually illegally.

Autonomous Semi-independent, with some powers of self-government.

Byzantine Empire Christian empire based in Constantinople; the Byzantines were successors to the eastern part of the Roman Empire and were conquered by the Ottomans in 1453.

Caliph Spiritual leader of the Muslim community; originally drawn from the Prophet Muhammad's circle, caliphs later assumed the lifestyle of emperors.

Cold War The war of words, ideas and propaganda between Communist countries and the western world between 1945–91.

Concession The right to use land, resources or industry etc, in a country, often to the exclusion of anyone else.

Coup (d'etat) Violent overthrow of a government or monarch.

Dynasty Family of hereditary rulers.

Elite Most powerful, rich or educated members of a community.

Empire Group of countries or people governed by one ruler.

Hegemony Supremacy of one state over all others, usually in a particular region.

Hijaz The western region of what is now Saudi Arabia, containing the Muslim holy cities of Mecca and Medina.

Ka'ba Ancient cube-shaped shrine in Mecca, once used by pagans but exclusively Muslim since the Prophet Muhammad's time.

Majlis Name given to an assembly (parliament) in various Middle Eastern countries.

Mandate Legal authority to govern a former colony, theoretically to prepare it for independence.

Martyrdom Suffering of a martyr, who dies for a noble, often religious, cause.

Mesopotamia Ancient name for the land between the Tigris and Euphrates rivers in present-day Iraq.

Mongols Asiatic warrior tribes unified by the military overlord, Genghis Khan, under whose leadership they conquered a vast Asiatic and European empire.

No-fly zones Areas in the north and south of Iraq in which the Iraqi air force was forbidden to operate in order to prevent attacks by Saddam Hussein against his enemies; the zones were patrolled by allied military aircraft.

One-party state Country in which only one political party is allowed to exist.

Ottomans Muslim dynasty based in Istanbul; ruled much of the Middle East until after World War One.

Persia Ancient name for Iran.

Protectorate Country which depends on another more powerful country for its military protection, and which is sometimes governed by that country.

Qur'an (Koran) Islam's sacred text; it is considered by Muslims to be the word of God as it is made up of the revelations given to Muhammad.

Regent Person appointed to rule in place of a weak or incapacitated monarch, for example, when a monarch is too young to take the throne.

Republic Country in which sovereignty is held by the people or their elected representatives, as opposed to the rule of a monarch.

Schism Division of a religion or group of people into opposing factions.

Secular Non-religious.

Shari'a Comprehensive system of laws and rules of conduct inspired by the Qur'an and the sayings of the Prophet Muhammad.

Shi'a, Shi'ism Minority branch of Islam which believes the succession to the Prophet Muhammad was unfairly taken over by those outside his immediate family. Shi'as form a majority of the population in Iraq, Iran and Bahrain.

Sunni Majority sect within Islam; Sunnis take their name from *sunna*, meaning 'the true path'.

INDEX